saying her name

poems by Margaret Van Every

saying her name
poems by Margaret Van Every

cover art and book design by Robert R. Burke

copyright © 2012 by Margaret Van Every

All rights reserved. Except for brief passages quoted in a newspaper, magazine, radio, or television review, no part of this book may be reproduced in any form or by any means, or by any information storage or retrieval system, without permission in writing from the author.

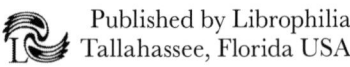 Published by Librophilia
Tallahassee, Florida USA

ISBN 978-0-9845025-2-3

Acknowledgements

The following poems, which appear in this volume, were previously published in the journals listed:

At Her Vanity, *Magnapoets*
The Pathological Liar's Support, *A Brilliant Record*
In Love, *Butterfly Away (Magnapoets Anthology Series 3)*
A Hospital Visit, *Many Windows (Magnapoets Anthology Series 4)*
Women in Their Kitchens, *Magnapoets*
That Special Time of Life, *El Ojo del Lago*
Crows' Feet, *Magnapoets*
Stone Soup, *Magnapoets*
The Bottom Sheet, *A Brilliant Record*

Several people have made valuable contributions to this book by way of encouragement, critique of content, and helpful suggestions. Among them I would especially like to recognize and thank Professor Neil Schmitz for his many fine observations; keenly perceptive poet and friend Jeanie Greensfelder; poet and mentor in Mexico, James Tipton; informed reader and appreciator Michael McGrath for his extraordinary guidance. A special thanks to writer and friend Zofia Barisas for her meticulous reading, suggestions, and introduction. I am also indebted to David Bryen and Ilsa Picazo for their assistance. Once again I am fortunate to benefit from the design and artistic support of Robert R. Burke of Tallahassee, Florida, whose work I so admire and who perfectly captures the spirit of the written word. One could not ask for a better team in putting together a book.

in memory of my mother
Myrtle Van Every Deutsch (1900-1951)

Introduction

Margaret Van Every's poetry is the poetry of family, of relationship with the other and with oneself, of joys snatched away, of loss, of yearning, of sadness. It speaks of sorrows, denial at first, then detachment, later empathy, compassion and love that carry us forward in the many changes from child to teenager to woman to mature woman to the beginning of cronehood and deeper wisdom.

The poet finds herself through the writing, and we, the readers, following her progress, revisit our own journeys that brought us to who we are.

The collection begins with *At Her Vanity:*

> . . . *I, her adoring*
> *subject, am audience at her feet, soaking*
> *this ritual up, a life lesson in what*
> *a woman does before she sleeps.*

These are the memories of a child watching her mother preparing for night—the beauty ritual a woman observes, offered up to her vanity. Multiple meanings, as in this title, occur in other poems, as do unexpected revelations as in *Drowning in Teacups:*

> *. . . a comforting cup of tea*
> *has sinister potential*
> *if we let down our guard,*
> *like the gentle hand of the family friend*
> *on whose lap we sometimes sat.*

There is acerbic wit and humorous takes on painful and serious situations and often a bleak view of cherished traditions. From *Sunset at Big Sur–A Nuptial Souvenir:*

> *and we go forth under a drab full moon,*
> *joined till death do us part,*
> *in search of enchantment.*

The beauty of language and the elegance of the metaphors recur throughout the book.

The writing frequently alludes to what is going on, rather than stating it directly, so that we fill in the picture with our experiences and it becomes our own. The poems bring us back to view our own life with an added dimension of depth and a sense of recognition of our shared humanity in the quotidian living of it.

The pivotal event here is a mother's death when the daughter is ten years old. The sadness at the loss is distilled through the beauty of metaphor where the aptness of the images softens the horror of the message. The music of the language alternates with direct statements, as when the father and the little girl return from the funeral:

> *we returned to the home she had made*
> *and never uttered her name again*

We are struck by the size of what this means. How is this possible? How could a husband and a child never mention her name again? The poem ends with an answer that brings death into the wider context of nature:

> *Or did we guess*
> *that if we spoke her name*
> *it would break the spell;*
> *our grief would spill*
> *like the riotous heads*
> *of condemned flowers*
> *adorning her grave,*
> *from their roots severed?*

We become part of that sadness and that renewal. The poem refers us back to our own lives, the universal become personal, the one reflecting the whole.

Margaret Van Every's poetry speaks of a happy childhood with a beloved mother with whom times of fun had to be hidden from a joyless severe father. The poems are saying her name over and over again, in the remembered times of complicity, and later in an acute awareness of her absence when her presence was so much missed in the growing up process.

It is a poetry sometimes of anger, always of endurance. The meaning sometimes expands, as in the abstract rendering in *Spinners*, into showing us whole internal parallel women's lives lived in freedom, while outwardly complying with the constraints of society's restrictions:

> *women spinning threads*
> *women spinning the sticky*
> *dew-bejeweled*
> *webs of fascination*
> *orbit by interior orbit*
> *spinning themselves*
> *into the center*
> *women enthroned*
> *awaiting peripheral tremors*
> *news from the border*

In the end what this poetry collection explores are the heart and soul travels of the motherless child who ambles forward as she must, on the sinuous path through puberty, love, motherhood, menopause, into old age, meeting obstacles and moving past. Through her eyes we get glimpses of other lives, the mother's, the father's, the bullies' at school, and so many others that touch her and are touched in return by who she is, in all her changing self. In this we see our own peregrination, our own search for certainty and home, always finding that certainty recedes and that home can only be reached when the search ceases.

She is given fullness of being, this woman long dead, who mothered for only ten years, whose daughter the poet brings back to life, from sitting at her feet as a child to writing the poem *It Is Good*, a poem with the flavor of a Japanese haiku in its last three lines, that uses nature to convey its message:

> *Crocuses*
> *bloom in winter*
> *through snow.*

There is, here, understanding and acceptance in the stated willingness to speak words of forgiveness, with the expectation that the heart must then follow. One looks back through the hope of this poem to all that came before, with now a gentler view.

And yet, with the resonance that the poetry evokes, Margaret Van Every writes as an outsider, the only motherless girl in school, the only one not allowed to wear make-up and nylon stockings, the one who plays the violin and is painfully shy. In writing from the outsider's point of view she mirrors the reader's times of separateness and aloneness.

The writing is like sea waves that take us out to her internal tides of feeling and bring us back to shore to once more look objectively at the word images that construct her reality. Past and present interlock to form an ever-changing landscape, as her growing understanding uncovers further nuances of what shaped her.

The poems mirror every aspect of the interweaving of our paths across the earth. The poet's painful reminiscences and explorations, and awareness of injustices suffered and inflicted culminate, in the last poem, *Crone*, in hard won wisdom and emerging quietude.

> i. Out of the cave
> *She stoops but not to please.*
> *Her hair is the color of roots,*
> *she wears black, hides nothing.*
> *Long ago she laid her burden down . . .*

Margaret Van Every's poetry reveals the paradox that many of us intuitively know—that we are not alone, that we share all human suffering and yet, our being separate from others in our solitary inner world is undeniable. The poems show, with courage, the poet's uniqueness that puts us in touch with our own and in this showing we are once more reminded that we are part of the whole.

Zofia Barisas
Ajijic, Jalisco

Foreword by the Author

Assembling this collection of poetry during the happiest time of my life has been an act of discovery for me, one that surprised me at first for the pain it evoked and later for the respect and awe I allowed myself in viewing my life's journey. Not until the assembling and editing were over did I realize that the book was not so much about me as it was a tribute to my mother, that her death in 1951 was in fact the beginning of my birth, it was then when I cut the umbilical cord and my own life began. There is a saying that everyone is born twice—once when your mother brings you into the world and again when your mother dies. My mother's death when I was ten was the seminal event in my formation. It colors the tone and content of nearly every poem in the collection.

It was in her passing that I understood at such an early age the harsh wisdom of just how solitary is the journey. We all must discover this sooner or later, mostly by trial and error or through the constant hammering we receive on the anvil of experience. Some are more fortunate than others in finding true teachers, partners, and wisdom without restless searching. Others, as in my case, tried and discarded much along the way. Only now, somewhat late in life, have I come to reside in a peaceful mental and physical space filled with light, a satisfying relationship, and immersion in a creative and appreciative community. I do not ask myself how I got here, but each day I revel in the palpable joy of my existence and the beauty and harmony that envelop me.

I ask the reader to consider these poems as testaments to the barbaric times in which many of us came of age. My mother died in 1951, when people used coping strategies of pretending, denial and repression, but never of processing loss. It was socially unacceptable to mention the word cancer or even acknowledge that someone was dying. There was no hospice or grief counseling. We children were instructed to "be little soldiers," which meant stoically shouldering our daily duties without dwelling on our loss. Since then there have been humane changes in attitudes toward the grieving process, child-rearing, housework, relationships, religion, menopause, and how women perceive themselves. In addressing many of these issues the poems have value as period pieces voiced from the contemporary perspective.

May you see something of yourself in these poems and join me in bringing your own journey to light.

Margaret Van Every
San Antonio Tlayacapan, Jalisco

saying her name

poems by Margaret Van Every

breaking the spell

breaking the spell

At Her Vanity

She sits in threes before the triptych glass,
perched on a needlepoint stool, applying
cold cream to a throat not yet lax with age.
She smears it on, rubs it in, then wipes it off
with tissue from a silver box. I, her adoring
subject, am audience at her feet, soaking
this ritual up, a life lesson in what
a woman does before she sleeps. At her
command, the tools of beauty lie: initialed
sterling comb and brush, a powder jar,
an atomizer. A hand-held mirror shows
her what she looks like all around.
One by one she pulls the tortoise pins
that bind her hair, the auburn coils unfurl,
drop like weights, are dealt 100 strokes.
Finishing touch: a simple pinch that sprays
intoxication through the air. She smells
good enough to sleep, perchance to dream.

The Fabled Boots

Those riding boots in the attic,
are they the legendary pair
a husband presumed to deny?
She wouldn't deign to beg and so
she mounted her steed bareback
and crop in hand galloped to a place
where she could buy her own boot.
Now at attention in the next husband's attic,
two sentinels stand at attention
awaiting the rider who never returns.

Her Hand

She'd dangle it behind the passenger seat,
sure that, like a ball of twine before a cat,
an encounter would ensue; her child would jump.
It seemed to me detached, that hand,
an entity apart from the rest of her,
a puppet with a life of its own.
I caressed it, kissed it, traced the blue
trees branching, stroked bones delicate
as fan ribs under vellum. I splayed
the fingers wide apart then lined them up again.
I knew the brown spots by heart, unvarnished nails,
half moons and ridges. Miles passed. I possessed
her through her hand and she gave it to me
unconditionally, though speechless, staring at farms
whizzing by. It was our secret. She let me turn
the golden band that bound her to our driver.

How Great Was Texas

Proud of Texas
and proud of her girls,
she packed us up in the '47 Chevy
and drove us clear to Texas
all the way from St. Louis
to show us Texas and Texas us.
We'd meet Aunt Minnie, Aunt Eva,
Great Aunt Pearl and Willa Anne,
plus a dozen cousins we never knew we had.
Then we could see for ourselves
how great was Texas.
The drive was long, hot, and dusty,
car windows rolled down,
socked feet hanging out,
hair whipping frantic in the wind,
past Burma Shave signs,
shacks with rockers and
wringer washers rusting on the stoop,
oil pumps bobbing like insatiable beasts,
cotton fields with cotton in 'em,
and she sang Dixie
with increasing abandon
the closer we got.

breaking the spell

Gas stations so few
we'd squat roadside in wildflowers,
car door for cover.
We were smitten with cowpokes and stallions,
Indians and cactus and mesas
in lurid sunsets. She took us to her hot spots,
a relative or two remaining in each.
Dallas, El Paso, Corpus Christi, Austin,
San Antone, Beeville, San Marcos. We saw
the Alamo, a rodeo, and crossed the Rio Grande
into Juárez with its silver charms and bangles.
We mingled there with people
neither white nor black.

Then noses to the north
we retraced our tracks,
a silent film in rewind.
We'd seen Texas and Texas us.

Mother could die in peace.

Mother Tongue

Her tongue was Texas
and though it had no drawl
it was foreign to her girls
who heard from other mothers
gentler tones.
Those mothers never
summoned their girls
with finger whistles,
nor was it in their
lexicon of persuasion
to shoot off commands like
hold your horses and pipe down.
She piped us down all right and
told us to keep our shirts on.
Then there was the N word
on her lips, which she'd say
sweet as you please
like nice day today
without a hint of denigration
and we'd do our best to set her straight
but she'd drawn her line in that Alamo
and wouldn't budge. That was
the Texas word for what they were,
nothing wrong with that at all,
she'd say, except in our heads.
It was only a word like table or chair
and we should never fear words,
and didn't we know sticks and stones
could break bones, but words
are mere vibrations in the ear.
We girls had a different sense
and knew that words could slice
but had no rhymes in our defense.

Mother Taught Us to Lie

When Daddy left town
we did the things
we knew he didn't want us to do;
we had to do them then
or not at all.

We had a party in the snow,
built snowmen and forts,
drank hot chocolate with marshmallows,
and all the children had a good time
and left no tracks.

We gave secret birthday parties
with hats and horns and little cups
filled with jellybeans.
Sometimes it was movies
and the Toddle House for dinner,
just us girls.

What we learned was
Daddy didn't like us having fun
but it was ok
as long as Daddy never knew.

Drowning in Teacups

It was like a bizarre factoid
from *Ripley's Believe It or Not*,
her revelation that
we could drown in a cup of tea,
and we had thought it possible
only in the ocean or swimming pool.
Without saying it she said
that something consequential
can occur in least expected places;
that a comforting cup of tea
has sinister potential
if we let down our guard,
like the gentle hand of the family friend
on whose lap we sometimes sat.

The Lure of Ice

Before she died, when I was ten, mother
warned us to never walk on glaciers.
This admonition, imparted as it was
from the middle of the Midwest, could only
have arisen from her own flirtations with the
lure of ice. She'd known firsthand how purity
attracts then swallows one whole.
                                    Now when
beckoned by a crystal road on a warm day,
I hear her words and decline the invitation.
I've turned away from ice caves in summer,
alpine flowers and frosty mist at the door,
cascades tumbling through the vestibule
to surface miles down slope.
                                   When I go near
the ice I hear a gentle descant above
the siren's song. I marvel how she had
the grace to warn us, how she knew.

Disownment

Threatening disownment
was the thunderbolt
she'd hurl if we dared depart
from her good-girl template.
She didn't have to define it
for we knew it meant
a total fall from grace,
expulsion from the garden,
excommunication from her love.

We'd be cast into dark woods
with no compass or crumbs;
banished to wander blind
the desert of disobedient children
or filthy city streets
at the mercy of strangers.

Okay, I said, when I was five
and ready to call her bluff.
Disown me if you want.
I'm running away.

Okay, said the Queen Bee,
I'll help you pack.

Rites of Passage

1. Before God

Get out of bed!
We'll say a prayer!
While we slept
she died he said.

We're on our knees,
eyes scrunched fast.
With palms pressed
and pointing up
we ask.

But we don't know
for what and
who's listening
or the structure of the thing
until amen;

and whether it's voided
if one of us peeks
or if we'll be laughed at
for doing this only
in emergency.

If there was a code
we weren't let in.
We'd never prayed
together before
and never tried it again.

2. Mute's Good-bye

For three years we could guess
but weren't allowed to ask;
when friends inquired
we kids were told to say
she's just fine, thank you.

She went as we her next of kin
lay soundly dreaming.
At dawn they phoned to say
her pain is over,
God took her,
where do we
send her now?
We let her go without
a touch or word,
for her or from her.

At the place they called "the home"
we came to say good-bye
and spend some time alone
with her as she lay in state.
I went up by myself
and thought hard the words
to make her somehow hear,
though seeing what was there,
I knew I was too late.

3. Saying Her Name

After our visitation at the mortuary;
after the eulogy was done;
after the lid was shut
and the pall borne out;
after the hearse transported the box
to Memorial Park
and the box was dropped in its bed
and covered with clods
and a blanket of flowers,

we returned to the home she had made
and never uttered her name again,
as though her leaving was
something unspeakably heinous
for which there was no forgiveness
or recompense.

Or did we guess
that if we spoke her name
it would break the spell;
our grief would spill
like the riotous heads
of condemned flowers
adorning her grave,
from their roots severed?

4. Memento Mori

A month of Sundays we'd drive to the Park
as though we had an appointment to keep.
There on the grassy mound we'd sit
and contemplate.

We're paying our respects, our father said,
and never did we ask what for,
but searched for the thoughts he wanted
of us at this place now.

We came to get credit for keeping the date,
as though it would somehow make her glad.
But would she know if we didn't show
and went to the movies instead?

Was she aware that I sat on her sod,
my feet tucked plumb with her head?
Could she feel the weight of her grieving child
compacting the earth on her lid?

In silence we'd offer tentative smiles
for having done the expected thing.
As though he needed the evidence,
he snapped our photo by the stone.

*. . . the merciful
whip
or absence
of wind*

. . . the merciful whip
or absence
of wind

The Father

He made two daughters.
They were not apples in his eye
but an orchard that took all his toil
and then he gave all the harvest away.

Duty, asleep in the blossom,
wormed its way into the core.
Without a harvest,
what was all the tending for?

Melting

He practiced the art
of masking where he was from,
but when his daughter
shrugged and flipped her palm
the coiled Hun-in-the-box
up-sprung and shook his fists.

When first he settled
on this new soil, he'd leapt
like a lemming into flames,
smelting the accent, gestures,
attire, trappings of the world
from which he'd come.

But after meltdown,
telltale dross remained . . .
like the child's hands talking.
So he issued his do's
and a litany of don'ts:

savor paprika and peppered stews,
but let your hands hang
like fishes that have gasped their last,
or fold them neatly in the lap,
still as an anesthetized cat.

Make others believe we're from here.

. . . the merciful whip
or absence
of wind

Young Actors

When the garage door rumbled
week nights at six,
a curtain fell,
a pall swept the boards.
We bowed to a phantom ovation,
put on straight faces,
rid the scene of all
props of improvisation
and prepared for
the coming act.

Rope

it arcs and drops
slaps the ground
arcs again and again
propelled by
the singsong chant
of girls in unison
chirping words
as automatic as group prayer

in the center of it all
a jumping girl
hops over the rope
keeps hopping
landing precisely
on the incantation's beat

like all who've jumped before
she keeps it up until she trips

... the merciful whip
or absence
of wind

Drill

After school bad boys
ran ahead and lay in wait
till we traipsed by
in galoshes and leggings,
scarves and mittens,
knit tasseled caps
and woolly coats,
clutching crayons, papers,
and lunch pails,
slipping and crunching,
foot after foot forward
lumbering toward slaughter.

Hating the bad boys,
cursing the school path,
despising the snow
flung in icy balls
while they, giddy,
laughed to score,

we trudged onward,
concealing our terror
under armor of indifference,
noticing nothing,
foot after foot forward
wending our way home.

Father and Daughter Make a Salad

He offers his back
for thirty seconds
as he turns to the sink
to scrub a carrot.
She with knife in hand
considers life in a cell,
how no one will believe
a child
and goes on slicing radishes,
red dye ravishing
the drain board.

. . . the merciful whip
or absence
of wind

Judy's Secret

Judy my best friend
in the fifth grade
pulled me close
on the wooden step
at the top of the stairs
where no one would see us
and made me promise
never to tell a soul
or I'd rot in hell
and I said I'd never.
She warned her father
could go to jail
if I told and again I said
I'd never.
Then with hot breath
she leaned into my ear
and said her father
the gynecologist did
abortions, which was
against the law. I said
I'd never heard of a
gynecologist or an abortion.
She said her father
killed unborn babies
their mothers didn't want.
I'd never thought about
there being babies
their mothers didn't want.

Mary Baker Eddy* Said

and many believed her
that we were never born
and therefore we'd never die
and we'd never be sick
between those nonevents
and we'd never celebrate birthdays
since we were never born
and never being sick
we'd never go to doctors.

And if you imagined
you were born or sick or dying
it was only a suggestion
of your nonexistent brain,
which she called mortal mind,
the tempter in the Garden
before the nonexistent Fall.

God had made us perfect
and so we couldn't sin.
Then hormones arrived and
we were attracted to
animal magnetism. Amen.

*Mary Baker Eddy founded the Christian Science Church in 1879. It is the church in which the poet was raised.

The Day I Spoke My Truth

*. . . the merciful whip
or absence
of wind*

The day I spoke my truth
was the day I told
Mrs. Priestly, the 6th grade
Sunday school teacher,
I thought God was bunk.
I didn't believe in the 6-day
creation or that I was made
in His image and likeness.
I didn't understand why
He changed His mind and
started over so many times
if everything He'd made
was perfect to begin with.
And furthermore I didn't
believe in prayer or that
anyone was up there
listening and granting,
for if He was omniscient
what was the point in our telling
Him what He already knew
and why would we propose
our own self-serving revisions
to His providential plan.

    I was relieved
after parting my own Red Sea
to plant my feet on the other
side. Now I could never go back.
I only regretted having caused
the tears that cut a moist path
down the powdered cheeks
of Mrs. Priestly, who had done
her damnedest to propagate
the myth, whose Goliath faith
was no match for a child's sling-shot
logic. Her Tower of Babel
aspiring to Heaven collapsed
and fell to pieces the day I
spoke the truth that set me free.

Seventh Grade

A head above her peers, the tall girl
stooped to be more like them.
She dressed like them in full skirts
and crinolines, slept on rollers
to achieve a pageboy curl like theirs.
She was the only motherless girl,
which made her strange until
she invented a mother to fill the gap.

But she was different in other ways,
schlepping a violin case
and wearing saddle oxfords
for dress-up shoes. Her father
wouldn't let her use lipstick
or stockings or hang out with boys
at the drugstore after school
for fear these things would
make her a woman too soon.

In stacks at the county library
she stumbled on sex in pages
of books that caused adults
consternation. She was the child
with early breasts, who monthly
bloodied her skirt, for no one
had told her how to know when.

She was the silent caller
who phoned her secret love
a hundred times only to hear his breath.
She was the girl who other girls
wanted to be like, who no one knew,
who harbored a sadness
impossible to share.

Ripe

*. . . the merciful whip
or absence
of wind*

Ripe too soon, neither woman nor child,
we reddened when traffic slowed,
dogs sniffed, and boys gawked and whistled.
The flesh in the mirror was nothing
we'd ever seen. We were Narcissus smitten
with metamorphosis, paying homage
for hours to the reflection, only vaguely
sensing what the changes implied.
From passed-around potboilers we got
a bent-page education that taught us that
passion happens in elevators and men steal
your clothes to hold you hostage
to their base instincts. I longed for the man
who would want me that much, who would
spare me the burden of the perfunctory no
and the moving aside of his hand. Where was
my Rhett to sweep me up the spiral stairs
of desire? Meanwhile I'd settle for the scrawny arms
of a boy my own age to enfold me in a slow dance
and simply kiss without conscience. We lacked
the gumption to say yes or ask would you.
But I could not wait; I poured my passion
into a shapely piece of resonant wood, my violin,
a responsive lover that ravished my heart.

We Are Wet Garments

hung out to dry
stiffening like cardboard
into form;
the shapes we assume
depend on how
we are pinned
and the merciful whip
or absence
of wind

the pas de deux

the pas de deux

We Knew Love When

We and we alone knew love
when time and technology conspired
for our delight. We came of age
on planet Earth in the blink of a
decade—after the Pill and before
AIDS—when gonads commanded
and folks responded unafraid of
the friction of skin against skin;
unafraid of uniting the invisible;
unafraid of mortal payment exacted
for unarmored ecstasy. A membrane
now seals the globe, securing flesh
from the hazards of touch.

In Love

I was a kite updrafted
let out to the end of the line
whose string was
released
whose exhilaration in clouds
was fatal
who couldn't differentiate
freedom from rejection

the pas de deux

The Pathological Liar's Support

His stories clung
like sprung underpants
afraid to fall,
suspended in part
by our credulity
to spare us
embarrassment and hurt.
But gravity's no fool
and took its toll.
When he lost his cover
we lost ours.

In Medias Res

As I am dying of typhoid
but don't know it,
I am laboring over the stove
and my husband and his friend
are grinding out their next book
on the dining table,
typewriters clacking,
papers strewn about.
Our three hungry boys
are clamoring
for dinner to be served.

Suddenly an explosion
jolts the room
into stunned silence
as a ball of fire
enters a high window,
whirls across the ceiling
and exits without a trace
through the open window
on the other side.

the pas de deux

Red Light Interlude

Waiting for the light to change, I glance
at the car idling in the adjacent lane.
The bearded man at the wheel,
white mop of hair, wild, uncombed,
unwashed like he'd just descended
from the mountain after a long retreat,
like me waiting for the light to change,
on his way to an obligatory somewhere.
In the passenger seat, a bored woman
twists a strand of hair, stares vacantly
into interior space. When the driver
looks at his watch with a certain shake
of his mop, I recognize the gesture,
then the man with whom I eloped
so many years ago, scorned by my family,
he disowned by his, we damned the world
and gave our all for love. For 17 years
we shared a bed, had three sons, and
I was the occupant in the passenger seat.
Now here we are, unwitting trio in the game
of marital chairs, almost within touching,
so close our brainwaves could collide.
As ever, he's oblivious and I feel nothing
but relief when the light changes
and all move on.

Cinderella at Age 50

After years of crashing balls in borrowed slippers,
if there's one thing I've learned, it's this:
men are like shoes.
Some you can break in, some you endure.
Those rigid as glass
you shed as you dash for the door.
Some you can live with, some you can't.
Alas, we never know until we try them.

The shoes of my life have sorely disappointed me,
but ah, how good they looked and felt when new.
In the end they hobbled me, every one.
The closet's full of them, barely worn.

Take wisdom, not heart, from this barefoot crone,
and shut your ears to ladies with wings;
If a prince comes calling with a shoe your size,
chances are slim it'll fit tomorrow;
and the maid who accepts the *pas de deux*
suffers the dance in a crystal shoe.

Sunset at Big Sur
A Nuptial Souvenir

The word's out—
a ritual death will soon be consummated.
Voyeurs gather on the strand
with their chicken legs, chips, and pop,
cameras, dogs, and babies.
Some disrobe to sop the radiant warmth
from sand and stone,
and all murmur the requisite
litany of clichés,
going blind trying not to look.
The congregation of the curious and prurient
faces west.

Trumpets blast through the piped dunes as
foam penetrates the rock,
gushes skyward;
rolls of pink surf spill sea bits
on the sand, recede to oblivion.

In a trice—and where were we?—
the dayglo oyster concentrates,
slips into the gaping maw.

So it is with high tragedy,
which often goes unnoticed
when we're straining to observe.

The cliffs are humble now,
devoid of copper sheen,
and we go forth under a drab full moon,
joined till death do us part,
in search of enchantment.

Chains

The Pakistani sales clerk
at the jewelry counter,
recently widowed,
counsels customers
on which chains
are good in bed.
Though not widowed
I have no one who'd notice
except perhaps to say
you've forgotten
to remove your necklace.

Prattle & Nonprattle

Because the husband believed that
words are an exhaustible resource
he saved them up for emergencies
only. Not long into the marriage he
ran out of everyday nouns and verbs,
not wanting to repeat himself, and
resorted to Roget's to say the
simplest things in a completely novel
way, which then was likely misconstrued.
Dwelling in silence and only thinking
used-up words, he communicated his
point with nods, shrugs, and grunts.

Because the wife believed that words
beget more words and you can't stop them
with guns or condoms, she always had
the floor, which was utterly vainglorious
since no one else wanted it. Worse still,
as time went on she noticed he wasn't even
listening, sufficient grounds for giving him
the silent treatment except it would only
have made him happy, and what would
become of them if both abandoned the
mounting burden of communication?

Although he couldn't find words to tell her,
he believed that ears are like blotters
that can absorb only so much, and also
that words once launched on the airwaves
never stop sending ripples through the
universe, clogging the invisible environment
and making it nearly impossible for future
historians to glean everything that was ever
said, once the technology for capturing and
sorting gone-by utterance is perfected.

Essentially, she was a believer in the
tree falling in the forest and making no
sound unless an eardrum vibrates in the
here and now, but what she really yearned
for was a response from anywhere after the
magnificent life form crashed to the forest floor.
Not an echo, but a dirge, sympathy, empathy, rage.

Word Glass

Time came when like an hourglass
emptied grain by grain
husband's every
word slipped
through the
slender
drain.
His words
all down, his
jokes, stories, beliefs
bottomed out, he couldn't
flip 'em for another go. Wife now
seized her chance and spoke for two.

the pas de deux

Codependents
(Balloon & Air)

Like it or not,
together they rise and fall.
Inspired,
that limp, amorphous blob
is puffed up expanded m ⁰ r p ʰ e d
into a perfect globe.
Away they fly together or not at all,
and the gas claims all the credit—
credit for form *and* levitation.
The modest membrane endures,
does its meditation:
hot air lends illusion
of   form
but   is   not   the   form.
The explosive expansive stuff
is mere vapor
unless it has an edge to push against,
a skin of restraint,
a wall beyond which there is
total   d i s s i   p a t i   o   n
into laughable flatus.

The Narcoleptic's Party
A Short Tanka String

The fish from its serving platter
flops onto terrace tiles.
The dinner guest says
Oh, wash it off,
we'll eat it anyway.

Chin fallen on chest
the narcoleptic at the table
digests his dreams
as others eat
pretending not to notice

how sleep snatched him
midsentence
over the line
between here
and . . .

While the host
takes five,
the dinner guest
steals the moment
to proposition the cook.

Party kaput,
the dinner guest splits,
household hits the sack.
The narcoleptic springs to life
now insomniac.

Loving Old Men

It's the old men,
the very old men,
whom I adore,
the ones who can flirt
flagrantly,
who've no more time to waste
or words to mince.
"Were I twenty-five
years younger I'd be
your perfect mate,"
they boast.

They send home-made valentines
and billets doux
that sound sincere,
penned in eloquent script
with no smudges or revisions.
The old men learned to
say it right the first time
and practiced penmanship
as boys with a scratchy plume.

They are wise and their wit
so cunning yet gentle,
I feel both joy and dread
to have them still.
My old men hug long
and press me to them hard,
kissing straight on the lips,
perhaps to hold back time
the way we did as kids.

Variations on a Theme

1. He Lost His Head

Atop a fencepost for all
to see, a dragonfly devours
her favorite after-sex snack,
namely her mate, which she
tackles—how else?—head first.
She finished him off then
finishes him off again,
a pick-me-up post-coital
delicacy plus insurance
against his philandering.

We know what was in it for her
but what did he think he'd get
out of poking his head down
that black hole? In quest of
an answer to an age-old
question, he forgot he had wings.

2. The Lady DF's Heady Lesson

Honey, didn't your daddy
ever tell you what you're
s'posed to do after
doing it?
(The ultimate sick
dragonfly joke.)

You've got another
inning, another hole
to play. Can't quit
now. Who knows,
maybe there's pleasure
to be had. Don't miss it.
You're good enough to eat.

3. Voice of the Dragonfly Child Within   *the pas de deux*

One highly overrated
fucking moment of bliss
taken on the wing and now
this absurd conclusion!
Who says I have to let her
munch my brains? Thanks,
I think I'll keep my head
when all about are losing
theirs. I have wings, don't I?

4. Voice of the Dragonfly Adult Within

We sires of the species
are proud to be of sacrifice
once we've been of service,
and uphold the honor of our
gender by submitting our
noble heads without question
to the intractable jaws of fate.

5. The Lady DF's Consolation

Ours not to reason why,
Daddy Fly.
Whoever made up the rules
must have known something
we can't fathom
from this fencepost.
Don't even try to
figure the sense
of it, just do as your
daddy and his daddy
did before.
      Question not the
inscrutable; injustice in
the facets of our eye
only proves a heaven.
Trust me. I've a feeling in
my gut you'll fly to your
reward. Bye, bye, Daddy Fly.

6. Daddy's Last Words

My darling, when you
yawn after we have sex
I get an irresistible
urge to look down
your pulsing throat.
Your mandibles are so strong,
your tonsils so gleaming.
I wonder if the rest of
your alimentary canal is
so   aesthetically   pleasing...

untutored geometry

The Annunciation

In billowing habit,
wings of her wimple magnificent in flight,
a nun flutters down the Renaissance stairs
of a hospital in Florence
where I wait with my husband in the lobby.
Radiant with news, she captures my hand
and fixing me in her cloying gaze proclaims
the lab confirms your womb is blessed.

Never will this bride of Christ imagine
the heresy that's rampant in my heart.
My womb is not a body part I'm wanting blessed
and were I not to be a mother by chance,
would I ever choose to be a mother at all.

The Natural Childbirth

Giving birth
I bit the nurse at my side
urging me to push
while the doctor waited
between my strapped legs
for the head to emerge
and the anesthetist threatened
to leave for lunch
if I didn't hurry.

Mouth dry as cotton,
I cried for water but none was given,
my only task the bearing down.
The doctor like a catcher
waiting for the pitch
shouted Mrs. Hodges hold still
as I tried to get off the table.

I breathed on cue
and kept bearing down,
back strapped flat.
I bore and bore,
light blinding my eyes,
mirrors out of focus.
Would I miss it, then?

Then the bursting, the tearing,
the fire in the canal;
all energy concentrated in the final push.
Contractions continued
as the man who delivered my first child
began to sew.

Not Mine

With music, candles, and wine
I'd planned to dine on the placenta,
the fresh one that lined my womb,
red and throbbing, recently rid
of the wee bones it fed.

Akin to liver and other organ meats,
it was supernutritious, this flesh
was mine, sanguine and lustrous,
possibly delicious, it tempted me.

The ancients always ate theirs,
though I never saw their recipes,
and aborigines still do, not to mention
most other mammals. Now it was
my turn. I needed it.

But when I asked the hospital
to refrigerate my placenta
until I could take it home,
they claimed it wasn't mine.
Upon entering the ward I had signed it away,
along with the baby's foreskin.

Later I learned they had freeze-dried
and sold it to a cosmetics factory
in France that extracted the hormones
for their fancy face creams.
That was the fate of my placenta
and yours, too, in case
you ever wanted to know
or write a letter to your congressman.

Savings

they bike home breathless,
faces and shirts stained with the day's play
and tell me they need to wash

and put on clean clothes
so they can return to the Baptist minister
and get saved,

and I ask my three urchins
haven't they been saved already?
They admit to many times

but why not be saved
as often as you can if it means only
washing your face and changing your shirt?

Their surplus salvations
are reserves in the bank in case
in a pinch they may need it

and I think how often
I've been saved myself, and the chances
of needing to be saved again.

The boys aren't much different from me
in that none of us knows for sure what it is
we're being saved from or for—

there's comfort believing we're covered.

untutored geometry

Women in Their Kitchens*

Today, leaning over the sink,
gnawing the last flesh
from the bone of the mango,
mango juice running down my arms,
I remember Janice,
last year or the year before,
making her colorful salad
of shrimps and mango,
leaning over the sink,
alone in her kitchen,
gnawing the last flesh
from the bone of the mango,
mango juice running down her arms.

are not alone

Earning Keep

Earn one's keep: to work in return for food and a place to live by doing what is expected.

Keep in this phrase refers to "room and board," which in former times sometimes constituted the only reward for working on a farm, in a home, etc.

A child's definition: it means take on responsibilities and do stuff around the house to show that u appreciate being taken care of and are not a waste of space, food and money!!

> The appropriate posture for earning keep
> is on her back or hands and knees
> or leaning over sink or stove
> or ironing board.
> No time clock tells her when to quit;
> her work is never done.
> She can't work long or hard enough
> to earn her keep and only she can guess
> how many children must be borne and fed,
> clothed, nurtured, nursed, chauffeured
> to satisfy her keep.
> No one else is counting.
> Only she knows how many meals shopped for,
> prepared, and cleaned up after;
> how many floors polished and windows washed;
> how many shirts laundered and mended.
> No payment, no value attached
> to work exchanged for keep.
> Her work is free and comes without a pension.
> Keep is a debt never satisfied;
> earning it, a state of mind.

untutored geometry

Mammary Sea

The ultrasound of my breast
on the overhead monitor
reveals a seascape
in rhythmic surge and break
the way the ocean crests and rolls
on a decently calm day,
steady in its pitch and drift,
adding up to a dependable sail.
It is so like a great body of water,
that sea inside my breast,
that I am rising and falling,
succumbing to motion sickness.
I have forgotten the lump
that set me adrift
and I ask the doctor how he explains
the Mammary Sea
with its wave and chop
and ominous shadowy depths
concealing a universe at war
with itself below the surface.
He replies that it only looks that way;
in reality, he says, the breast
is composed mostly of fat.

Secret Griefs

We knew boys had something we were missing,
but hadn't a clue that we'd get something they
would lack. Mothers guarded their blood waste
in child-proof cans, stifled questions, saving up
the mystery till minutes before our own debut
to womanhood.
                      The prevailing rule
appeared to be that those doing it preserve
the secret from those who were not. Magazines
referred to "those days" as though only
initiates knew what days they were talking about;
we despised their coy euphemisms,
preferring the street name. We knew a curse
when we saw one.

                      From secrecy we intuited shame,
something akin to bathroom matters or why not
talk about it? One thing was certain,
our bodily functions were out of control,
making us tie on something like diapers to save
us from disgrace. The precocious formed a society
of secret sharers and hid their shame, while those
who started late suffered the shame of exclusion.

Resentment and tears accompanied the first strapping
on of the belt, an elastic harness to tame
our wildness, though wildness of another sort
ensued. Then grief, for *what* we couldn't fathom.
We only knew our lives advanced a notch
without our blessing. We weren't the girls we thought
we were before.

untutored geometry

    Thirty years hence we prick
our ears to hear what happens next, just
before it happens, of course. Mothers guarded
this one, too, speaking of "the change" while sweating
and fanning their faces in winter. The real word for it
they never uttered aloud, for it was the vaguely
shameful secret of women to whom the label
applied. Losing the monthly cycle was something
like being unsexed or neutered, a badge
of obsolescence. Now ad men call it "that special
time of life," flattering women exhausted
of eggs into buying the pill of postponement.

Some say that after the unused napkins are
forgotten, only the unmedicated crone knows
who she is. In some lands she wears black, her way
of telling the world she's not in mourning but is through
bleeding and doesn't give a damn.

Spinners

i.
women spinning threads
women spinning the sticky
dew-bejeweled
webs of fascination
orbit by interior orbit
spinning themselves
into the center
women enthroned
awaiting peripheral tremors
news from the border

ii.
women dropping anchor strands
swinging free
women crafting
the untutored geometry
of entrapment
whiling the day away
in the eye of the hammock
sipping dewdrops
waiting for a knock at
the periphery

iii.
women in their prime
ceaselessly spinning the
silken filaments of expectation
the strongest stuff known
women mummifying
friendly callers
in bullet-proof body bags
women sipping ichor
dining on *papillon en papillote*
alone
in their own sweet time

untutored geometry

iv.
women spinning
contriving to the end
the concentric
architecture of survival
tired, persistent, tangled
in the stickiness
of the world's strongest
substance
women centered
sending vibrations
to the periphery
damning the centripetal
enthroned at the center

Mme. Bovary Today
(as seen on The Divorce Court)

The lady's husband wanted to dump her
because she had 18 credit cards
and had run up a debt of $75,000.
Addicted to shopping
she said she couldn't help herself because
her husband worked all the time
and paid her no attention
so she hoped that clothes would make
him (or someone) notice her
but all he noticed was
the bills and unwashed dishes piling up
though he should have known,
as did Flaubert back when
there was credit but no credit card,
that women wived to the house
seek solace in shopping
and in lovers who pay mind to
what they wear, especially when it comes off,
and in that giddy moment they don't care how much it cost
because the cuckold, who had it coming, paid the bill.
Husbands can't comprehend
the triangle in the marriage:
them, the lady, and shopping.
Then one day she eats rat poison.

that special time of life

Crows' Feet

Squint, they warned,
and you'll get crows' feet,
but we scoffed and thought it silly
until the day we woke to find
the crows had landed,
not as we frolicked in the sun
but while we slept they stepped
across the temple corners of our eyes,
lightly so as not to waken
and left their print.

That Special Time of Life

Egg cells peak numerically during the embryo's 20th week of gestation at around 6 or 7 million, after which they dramatically degenerate and decline in number throughout a woman's life. Only about 500 cells are actually used for potential fertilization, and at menopause only a few thousand remain.

>Since peddlers caught wind that menopause
>is a market, they've coined a pretty phrase for it—
>that special time of life. What's special about it
>is that a woman runs out of eggs and her body
>runs amok when all the eggs are gone.
>Does she miss the eggs? Hell no, she never
>saw one unless the thing was zapped.
>For forty years she'd see the bloody wash
>that flushed the eggs away, the corks and rags.
>Nonetheless, some say she grieves when all
>the eggs are gone—grieves she'll see the bloody
>messenger no more, grieves for lost potential.
>
>But this is a special time of life, they say. Could this
>be what they mean: for want of estrogen her bones
>will thin, her back bow, her privates atrophy,
>and she may be incontinent, a fancy word
>for needing diapers. Flashes, sweats, and migraines,
>too, make this a special time, but not to worry,
>she's not sick, she's changing. Hairs on her head
>may take a mind to go and leave her bald; those
>hanging on, lose luster, turn gray. Whiskers will sprout
>where never seen before. Wrinkles, wens, and spots
>will force character on this woman's face, before so bland.
>Her arteries will harden, mental functions blur, and
>equal at last with men, she'll be at risk of heart
>disease in all its forms.

that special time of life

During this special time,
if husband or lover views The Change with patience,
sex could be a blast, there being no concern
for pregnancy or need for prophylaxis. Children grown
and gone, the bedroom's finally safe for sex,
the sanctuary dreamed of all those years. The problem
is, the lady out of eggs may be out of something else—
desire, because 'twas hormones all along that made
her like it so and now she can't seem to give a fuck,
plus the man in question may not find the sagging
flesh and shriveled parts appealing. So, what's
a man to do that has his own depletion woes,
running out of juice and jazz, running out and down?

Take heart. You see, it's his special time of life
as well. This simultaneous coming apart is part
of nature's plan for golden years. How sweet it is
to come of age together and fall downhill like
Jack and Jill, hand in hand, and laugh the whole
way down—that is, till someone breaks a crown.

The White Orgasm

like the white lie,
by its pallor less than the real lie,
a deceit forgiven on delivery
because it benefits the deceived,
is for his own good
to spare him something,
if only self-esteem.

He's wearing out his knees,
elbows, haunches, fingers, tongue,
but on his Code of Honor
cannot call it quits until she's satisfied.
He cannot comprehend
that quitting is the satisfaction craved.
He cannot rest until she oohs and aahs
and calls to God.

She tries imagining they're someone else
or younger versions of themselves,
humping in the dunes or in the car.
She plays the mental games
that used to yield results,
but now her mind meanders
to tomorrow's dinner and what
she needs to buy. Truth to tell
she's sore down there and tired all over.
She'll never reach the end; she's only
trying not to fall asleep before he's satisfied.

He's programmed not to quit until she comes.
It's not her fault; the more she tries
to will it, the more the brink recedes.
She's old. She yawns. She's going fast,
not coming. Now's the moment
for release of least resistance.

O God, she sighs and shudders,
moans and writhes and rolls her eyes.
At last, in faux post-coital bliss,
they're finding satisfaction in the other's arms,
legs and dreams entwined.

Absent Without Leave

that special time of life

Our dear friend is vanishing,
absent though among us still.
She began dropping clues
a while ago, retelling anecdotes
word for identical word.
And we would always
feign surprise anew, as though
we were hearing it for the first time.
And if she didn't know she was
repeating herself, maybe we too . . . .
How would we ever know, our friends
conspiring in the name of courtesy
to deceive us? Yet more and more
she'd forget her purse or misplace
her keys; then she'd lose the car
and next her way.

          They study her brain,
pronounce her normal, while we
who love her see she's taking
leave. She's in a hurry now
and won't wait for their scans
to catch up with her.

Stone Soup

Science has found a way
to insert a probe in the brain
like a spoon in a stew and
stir stuck bits from the bottom,
and none too soon for me,
for my details are vaporizing,
making bland the spice
that seasons reminiscence.
My sister's past has already
slipped beyond her grasp,
rendering me sole keeper
of our shared childhood.
Now she denies ever knowing
the stuff too tough to swallow,
and I am the mother of invention
as well as an only child
waiting like a watched pot
for a spoon.

Breath

Brightness falls from the air—Thomas Nashe (1567-1601)

The luminescence I have so long sought
surrounds me in the air I've breathed
since the welcome slap
that triggered the first gasp and cry;
all along it was this brightness
infusing my being with every inhalation.

The unacknowledged miracle:
we breathe and life goes on.
The old is traded for the new and fresh,
the invisible food that nurtures every cell
exchanged for the poison inside—
and all unbidden.

So simple I might have missed it
until that day I struggled for air,
drowning in myself;
it was then I acknowledged
the gift of luminescence
and offered thanks for the life I knew
when breath visited on its own,
without invitation.

A Hospital Visit

I enter the dim room in the rehab center
and delineate the shallow contour
of pillows on the bed
and I think oh they've taken her
for a test or physical therapy
but as I near the bed the pillows shift
ever so slightly and I discern
the frail form of the one
I've come to see, my friend of
thirty years, a shrinking heap of bones
bundled in a fetal crescent, awaiting
delivery. I take her birdlike hand,
stoop to kiss her brow. I've
brought her Vogue to take her back to
who she is inside, to let her know
the obscenity of the hospital gown
can't conceal the lady of fashion,
but all for naught. She can't read today
for her eyes are blinded with tears
of epiphany. The light she sees is
more painful than her ribs dissolving
under pressure when she turns in bed—
that though her friends are many
and she has the love of children,
she is alone.

that special time of life

A Death/A Birth
she prays to Death to take her soon

in morphine haze she sees
her long-gone Shermie
arms outstretched
to lift her
over the threshold

she comprehends
that dying's such a bore
for those
condemned to wait
without benefit of coma

family arrive
to wait with her
in the airless, twilit room,
fighting the impulse to doze,
avoiding words that need saying

a charade:
shadows drift in,
buzz in undertones,
eat her untouched lunch,
exit on tiptoe

no one ever taught her
the art of peaceful dying—
useful knowledge
applicable
just once

she's ready—
nails enameled, hair coiffed,
her trademark orange socks
on feet that can't take her
anywhere she wants to go

pointing at the pillow
she asks me
would you?
I would have had I thought
no one was looking

fetal curled
she waits to be delivered,
having long since said farewell.
Please, someone, come cut the cord
binding her to this worn out womb

Fast Forward

You've picked up speed
so imperceptibly
you're exceeding the limit
unawares,
not that your foot is leaden,
mind you, you just
can't seem to gauge
acceleration
by the increasing blur
of objects
outside your window
or the rate at which
stuff you've left behind
vanishes in
the rear view mirror.
If only it were so
that those we love,
now specks in the rear view,
were closer
than they seem.

The Shortest Day

the day is too short
to heat up the iron
to answer the IRS
to reply to email
to on-line shop
to make an appointment

the day is too short
to wash your face
to file your nails
to floss your teeth
to finish the chapter
to make a to do list

the day is too short
to say not now
to say later
to say a prayer
to finish the argument
to maintain the illusion

The Bottom Sheet

is averse to corners,
rounds three, balks at four.
Each year it resists the more,
strengthens as I decline.
One day I shall lose the match,
lay me down on mattress ticking
ticking time.

Memorial

It was a celebration for Jim
but I grieved for Arthur
my friend who left us at age 83.
Died of a worn-out heart, he did.
Arthur said it was a damn shame
the deceased couldn't listen in
at their own funeral on all the things
the mourners had to say about them,
those sentiments people save
for saying only after you're gone,
as though it'd be too embarrassing
to say them to your face,
and so I offered to provide a service
for Arthur before he died
so he could hear from his pretend coffin
how we cherished and would miss him,
but Arthur declined for fear that
it would look like he was starved for love,
begging for praise before its due.

His wife buried him under an oak
in the back yard, with no one there
but herself and the daughters,
and so when Jim's ashes danced
on the gold-flecked lake at sundown
and the revelers let fly the balloons,
it was Arthur on my mind.

It Is Good

It is good
to say *I forgive*
before you mean it;
your mouth has a head start
but in time
the heart catches up.
Crocuses
bloom in winter
through snow.

Crone

i. Out of the cave
She stoops but not to please.
Her hair is the color of roots,
she wears black, hides nothing.
Long ago she laid her burden down,
travels light enough to fly.
Hunchback, there's wisdom in her pack,
she's toothless, warts and wens,
a whisker prairie on her chin.
She burned her bra,
can't make a child if she wanted to,
doesn't want to.
Your drama, she's lived it.
It'll pass. It's a rerun.
Like her, revise, write a new script.
Unearth who you are.

ii. Why she loves chiaroscuro
out of darkness, light
from the shadows, blinding brightness
from the deepest depths, brilliance

iii. What the trials taught her
Judge not.
Be selfless yet love yourself.
Practice compassion.
Laugh.
Love.